STANDING ROOM ONLY

A COLLECTION OF POEMS

BY

DERMOT FRANCIS McGARTHY

Printed in Victoria, Canada

Note for Librarians: a cataloguing record for this book that includes Dewey Classification and US Library of Congress numbers is available from the National Library of Canada. The complete cataloguing record can be obtained from the National Library's online database at:
www.nlc-bnc.ca/amicus/index-e.html
ISBN 1-4120-2913-9

TRAFFORD

This book was published on-demand in cooperation with Trafford Publishing. On-demand publishing is a unique process and service of making a book available for retail sale to the public taking advantage of on-demand manufacturing and Internet marketing. On-demand publishing includes promotions, retail sales, manufacturing, order fulfilment, accounting and collecting royalties on behalf of the author.

Suite 6E, 2333 Government St., Victoria, B.C. V8T 4P4, CANADA
Phone 250-383-6864   Toll-free 1-888-232-4444 (Canada & US)
Fax 250-383-6804   E-mail sales@trafford.com   Web site www.trafford.com
TRAFFORD PUBLISHING IS A DIVISION OF TRAFFORD HOLDINGS LTD
Trafford Catalogue #04-0741   www.trafford.com/robots/04-0741.html

13   12   11   10   9   8   7   6   5   4   3   2

ABOUT THE AUTHOR

Dermot McGarthy was born in Dublin in 1963.After graduating from University College Dublin in 1987, he moved to London, where after a brief sojourn in banking, he began teaching English, and indulged his greatest passion-travel. Teaching assignments brought him to Eastern and Southern Europe and ultimately to Seoul in South Korea, where he taught Economics and Political Science. The intrepid voyager returned to his native shore in 1996.Dermot began writing short stories in his teens and has had some of these published in individual collections. He began to seriously pursue the craft of poetry over the last 5 years. This is his first collection. Dermot currently lectures in Communications Studies at the Dublin Institute of Technology.

THIS BOOK IS DEDICATED TO MY MOTHER,

MARY JOSEPHINE REYNOLDS.

FOREWORD
BY
PETER KAY

I first met Dermot McGarthy in Walter's Lounge in Dun Laoighre, where a mutual friend introduced me to him in late 2000. Soon afterwards Dermot and I agreed to meet at Bewley's Cafe, Westmoreland Street. My early impressions of Dermot were not unduly favorable. He paid scant heed to a poem I read for him and I took him to be self-obsessed. But we agreed to meet again and then I began to make a remarkable discovery. Here was a man with an extraordinary extrovert personality combined with inner vision and largesse of spirit capable of encompassing the entire universe. We soon became firm friends and ever chose to regard each other as brothers in God.

In early 2001 we traveled together to Copenhagen and the great energy of Dermot propelled us both to places I might never have reached, had I journeyed on my own. To travel with Dermot is always an adventure. We met often during the year and Dermot began to show me some of his poems. Here, I knew instantly was a poet who was going to go far.

At the end of 2001 we traveled to New York together. Before we went, he gave himself the name of 'Lantern Red' and I gave myself the name of 'Lantern Green'. We had a whale of a time over the Christmas, staying in the house of a kind friend, Peter Rosenberg, in New Rochelle, just north of New York City. It was a strange time to be in New York because the events of 'Nine Eleven' were fresh in peoples' minds and when we went to visit the Ground Zero site, it was still emitting smoke.

Dermot and I both found New York to be an inspiration for our poetry. Although he is a late starter in the poetry game, Dermot has worked conscientiously at his craft and has now gathered together enough poems for a first collection.

I like to think of myself as a traveler, but Dermot is the traveler par excellence. He has lived in London, Greece, Prague, Bilbao, and Seoul, and visited North Africa, several countries in South America, Hungary, Bulgaria, and Japan. Wherever he goes, he meets and greets. He believes that "God abides in the traveler."

I would say that our relationship has been stormy at times, what with my somewhat obsessive and perfectionist personality and Dermot's outgoing and expressive energetic whirlwind of a mind. Nevertheless we seem fated to be friends for life and – hopefully in the next world, in which we both ardently believe.

The poet, Percy Bysshe Shelly, has said that poets are "the unacknowledged legislators of their race." I have felt –increasingly so in the circa three years that I have known him-that Dermot is destined for great things. He is a man who is going to accomplish something that will be remembered forever.

Dermot has been a teacher for the past fifteen years and, amongst other things has taught history. I once wrote to him "May you not merely teach history, but become part of it's unfolding tapestry." This is my earnest wish and heartfelt wish prayer for the life of Dermot, a man who squeezes every moment like a lemon and zestfully drinks the juice.

As a person who would rather comprehend a spiritual cosmos than live in a religious cage, Dermot's rich sense of humour, combined with a deep empathy for all who are suffering in the world, mark him out as a man among men. He never allows his great intellectual prowess to overrule the deep observations of the compassionate eye of the heart. Some people have turned from him because of what can seem, at first sight, to be a brusque manner. This may be their greatest mistake.

It is now time for me to graciously bow out and commend to you the poems, which will speak for themselves. Salutations and congratulations to a dear and beloved friend.

PREFACE

Welcome to "Standing Room Only", The poems herein deal with a variety of commonplace human emotion and experience-love, loss ,sex, acceptance, obsession ,forgotten youth ,art, heritage, history, death, eccentricity, alienation, misused tradition, racism, personal internal conflict, commercialism, hope, despair, delinquency, complacency, begrudgery, temptation, sanctuary ,a wonderful river, and the omnipotence of Time. The singular theme running throughout all of this work, is of course, the power of the spirit and the crucial and overriding role that spirituality plays in all of humankind's endeavors, be they simple or complex.

Patrick Kavanagh was of the opinion that God made only geniuses, but that not everybody liked God's work. This gem of wisdom from my favorite poetic craftsman provides a backdrop as to why I decided to create this book in the first place,- namely to contribute to the human cache of function and dysfunction. More pointedly, to examine, confront, reflect, assess, validate, document, affirm and dissect the human condition from cradle to grave and beyond. This is merely the duty of any poet and is, in it's essence, the artistry of poetry itself.

The role of the audience in this context is to partake of the grand experiment, to follow the route, which the poet has journeyed, to travel from poem to poem, from highlight to lowlight. The reader will smile, laugh, grimace, cry, be moved to anger, be swayed towards compassion, and most importantly the reader will listen, listen to the rhythm within the rhyme.

As far as any art form represents itself, and more specifically- within the context of relationship between poet and reader, it is never a question of like or dislike of the material, nor is it ever a question of agreement or disagreement with the writer .It is merely, yet most definitely, a question of understanding, and if the reader has any duty at all then it is exactly this-to understand.

The poet is, and must by natural design be forever an outsider- an observer. It is in this sober and oft times austere landscape of isolation that *inspired objectivity* is more readily obtainable. Life as seen through this writer's eyes is a vast collection of heartbeats, and when these beats are all used up we must move on. All creative people are by definition spiritual. It is from the spirit that we all emanate, and one day near or far, we shall be safely delivered. Back to the spirit world .In the meantime, until that eventuality occurs, it's important to keep in touch, so to speak.

DERMOT FRANCIS McGARTHY

DROGHEDA,
APRIL 2004

REJOICE NOT IN HIS DEFEAT YOU MEN,
FOR THE BITCH THAT BORE THE BASTARD IS IN HEAT AGAIN.

EDGAR ALLEN POE.

LOVE'S MERRYGOROUND FOREVER KEEPS ON SPINNING, LOSERS HANG ON, THINKING THEY ARE WINNING.

DERMOT FRANCIS McGARTHY.

HAPPINESS IS A HOW, NOT A WHAT, A TALENT, NOT AN OBJECT.

HERMAN HESSE.

Poems In Order Of Appearance.

1) Waiting For........?
2) Standing Room Only.
3) Prisoner.
4) Tempted.
5) City Lights.
6) All Roads.
7) Boyne Poem.
8) For Lloyd and Jeanette.
9) Hotel Lullaby.
10) Exhibit A.
11) Borders.
12) Where To Now?
13) Love Thief.
14) Delirious Captives.
15) Destiny's Choice.
16) For Joey Ramone 1951-2001.
17) Party Time.
18) Round Trip.
19) The Mermaid.
20) Stopwatch.
21) The Good Land.
22) One Hundred Thousand Welcomes.
23) Hanging Tough.

24) Playback.
25) Hidden Eye.
26) Love's First Song.
27) The Unfortunate Cup Of Tea.
28) Lightening Strikes.
29) Departure.
30) Shadow Boxing.
31) Rainbow's End.
32) City Of The Dead.
33) Face To Face.
34) My Mother Is In Love With Gregory Peck.
35) Inner Sanctum.
36) One Voice.
37) Stranger.
38) Homeward.
39) Southbound.
40) Top Of The Morning.

Waiting For.............?

Time has no lasting effect,
Except to say that it is sorry,
For it's actions.
For imposing restrictions,
Permitting afflictions, with new pressures,
Playing hardball with old addictions.

Heartbeats, strong and faint,
Rejection, denial, immovable constraint.
I have seen it in the faces of the powerful,
I have watched it pour from the eyes of the
poor.
Time seduces with sweet discretion, one
billion guises,
Leading you through that open *Door*.

16

Standing Room Only

When you die and go to Heaven,
You know you will never be lonely,
All of life's passions residing there,
Standing room only.

<u>Prisoner</u>

There is a distance in your eyes.
Like the giant cast-iron *Golden gate*,
Connecting all the *wherefores* to the
whys?.
You yearn for contact,
To feed an abandoned soul.
A once proud nature, now entombed.
Waiting for discovery,
Like some Dead Sea scroll.

Tempted

Swivelling, Swirling, Surly, and Sullen,
It casts it's magnetic glare,
Falling heavy, down upon my fragile orb.
Like hailstones on a summer's day,
A gritty, biting intrusion,
Sudden and without warning.

This blazing orange power,
With the fevered din of ten football fields,
Summons me to attention.
Like a beacon, in a broad edifice of brown
and grey,
With large feet, I have overstepped the
nebulous mark.
I have fumbled my way into its snare.

CITY LIGHTS

With neon arms outstretched,
Cradling to its bosom,
One million heartbeats.
Success and failure frolic together.
Each has a part to play.
This Rome is re-built every day.

Looks of anger, looks of loss.
Painful decisions made at the toss.
Ploughing the furrow, searching for the
seam.
Recreating histories on which we all lean.

If Time itself had a museum,
What are the riches therein we might
glean?
At the parlour of fantasy, in the hall of
second chance,
Would the music be different?
Would we dance the same dance?

From spires on high and walls of stone,
Through sturdy oaks and gallons of foam,
Time, our conqueror, puts us to the sword.
City lights remain ageless,
Our spent years they hoard.

All Roads

This is the terminus,
Within these walls, where shadows divest
themselves.
In the corner, fantasy hides it's head
shamefully.
One tear, like a tree in a forest, falls.
Then another and another,
Until all the years crash in unison,
To thunderous applause.

Lying two together,
In our shroud of beaded sweat.
We are voracious readers,
As we thrall through this library of Time.
Tripping each other with our playfulness,
Laughing off the other's haunting spectres,
Jousting with fate, and losing every time.

We have arrived at the crossroads, where
all roads lead to.
We have paused at the point, where all
journeys commence.
Reeling, in the remoteness,
In this sacred hiding place, inhospitable to
future and past,
We covet a sneak preview of the final
destination.
As we return to the fray,
Through a secret door, found in each
other's eyes.

Boyne Poem

No thundering cliffs of wild heather here.
But dreamlike nature, suave, genteel and
seductive.
Ripples of blue in the wide expanse,
Concealing imaginary salmon , swaying
water lilies,
And souls, who ended their earthly
journey,
In the syrupy undercurrent.

She is proud of her long life,
Her place in a small nation's history,
A sacred keeper of bloody secrets and
nefarious deeds.
Cradled in the arms of this county Louth
town,
Her escort to the sea, and witness to an
unfading beauty.
In timeless majesty, for generations past,
and yet to come.

<u>For Lloyd and Jeanette</u>

In this cradle of spirits, in this cauldron of
tears,
Your life force reverberates through this
prism of years.
Embedded in flesh, cast in stone
Hanging on walls, the past is on loan.

For time is meaningless now,
No suitor for your human passions
Rather the rolling meadow, the lush
summer orchards
The wide gaping Hudson, will remain
A timeless testament to your onward
journey.

32

Hotel Lullaby

A lost and restless heart newly born,
Beating in the bare morning air.
The sole activity of this deserted body.
Emptied of all its human cache,
Long and lite, cobra-like,
Stretched out upon a flat scaly belly.
Entangled in crumpled sheets, and brightly
coloured eiderdown,
Still warm with lovers scent.
The tingling fragrance besmirched by one
solitary teardrop,
Falling slowly upon the satin stage.
A mind like an Olympic sprinter racing in
rapid tempo.
Striding desperately towards the finish
line, still out of sight.
His stomach flutters to a seagulls squawk,
Summoning early morning brethren
outside a bay window.
Waves lash against the rock, meters below,
Roaring back their approval.
As if all nature was part, of the same
wonderful orchestra,
The same sinister conspiracy.
Entombed in this barren interlude,
He wished he were a seagull.

But he could not be part of that creation,
For seagulls were never alone.

Exhibit A

History has your name filed away, under
"*misfit*".
Even mathematicians can't figure you out.
For future centuries' procurement, it's
better that it should be this way,
That you shall remain,
A secret to all those who never knew you,
An enigma to all those who did.
Always a mystery to yourself,
On your loud and raucous journey, to some
promised salvation.
An artefact, as yet unborn,
Of troubled times in a turbulent age.

BORDERS

How far before this road bends? The child
enquired.
How far until we reach the sea, until it
cradles us with its dazzling
smile of liberty? The mother mused
How far, How far ,How far?

Deep within our deepest creation, we
search,
To scale the summits of our lives, and then,
To leap from these same summits,
To replenish our empty caskets of time,
To drink from these barrels,
Until all reason is lost, and,
Reason found again.

How much farther will this road take us?
Is it as far as the distance that hate creates?
Or is it as near as the love a generous spirit
reveals?
We will travel this route, all the way to the
end,
Until we reach ourselves, and then,
Stop.

WHERE TO NOW?

Up a ladder, down a snake,
Better run for your life, jump in the lake,
When smart-assed meets sanguine,
In this game of give and take.
Reach for the stars, follow your own,
To history's final confluence,
Where your rebel heart still beats alone.

Your soul is most at rest, where ancient
waters lap.
The spirits of the vanquished,
Gushing from the tap.
A promise of a second chance,
This yearning for a life re-born,
Where emptiness is everything.
An eternal longing, forever and forlorn.

LOVETHIEF

Always a need to know, never any need to
care,
Secret wardrobes, you will lay them bare.
Gardens of Eden ,you will purge,
When honour smiles in your direction,
The devil will force-feed you the urge.

Your heart beats for failure,
For causes lost not won,
Hunting down noble ambition,
Running scared from the sun.

Your fund of dreams is bankrupt,
Your moral credit, long since run out.
Good fortune of others knaws at you
A niggardly, mean –spirited, negative life-
force,
Turning itself inside out.

Delirious Captives

When Time changes tears into maudlin
ether,
When it forgives everything and forgets
nothing.
When we have come so far,
We want to retreat swiftly from the
precipice,
To run, and to jump headlong into the great
vastness.
Of this,
Our own precious pleasure zone of self-
delusion.

Our minds are lofty heights,
Reeling upon scaffolding, shaking in its
very foundation,
Forever fragile.
We can see farther now than we could ever
see before,
Peering out from this perch of smug
elevation.
Delirious captives,
Looking in one direction only
Backwards.

Destiny's Choice

From this warm heart, where passions lie,
I build a ladder to the sky.
Seeking the one who comes from afar,
I call His name from every star.

Silence is the sole riposte,
Darkness or light at destiny's toss.
The choice is made, I must progress,
Through the ruptured mire, of life's
distress.

To stand alone, to speak His name,
To hear it's echo, it's doleful refrain,
On every face in every street,
Where the dead, the dying, and the undead
meet.

A message is sent, a pact is made,
Oh children of light, be yee not afraid.
Your course is chartered, your fate is
sealed.
Where honest hearts are beating, devotion
is revealed.

For JOEY RAMONE
(1951-2001)

The scrubland jingle jangled between
Forest Hills and Flatbush Avenue.
You gave it a voice, and you were its echo.
From Rockaway Beach and the High
Schools,
To teenage heartbeats all over the world.

In Rock Heaven there is a new star.
A beacon forever shines,
Between Van Courtland Park and Flushing
Meadows,
On Sheena who is still a punk rocker.
A thriving energy in her soul,
An innocence of diamond blue in her eyes,
And someone whispering softly into her ear
'Baby I love you'.

Party Time

For romantic fiestas, bloated bank holiday
siestas,
Festivals of dubious excuse.
Post religious ceremony,
Plied with children ugly or bonny,
For funeral parties, our fees we can reduce.

The emphasis is on laughs,
We don't do things by halves.
Laugh or cry, there's nothing in between.
With liquor of the best, please take it on the
chest.
Our "Bill of Fare" is like nothing you've
ever seen.

DJ Dave is a likely lad,
Specialising in the latest fad.
He can slow it down or speed it up just
right.
Remember when and where ,for real or for
a dare.
Because they're worth it, you can wallow in
the light.

When your wallet's flat,
You take off your party hat.
You sweat and toil, for a chance to shine
again.
Your conscience will be swayed, by he who
hasn't paid.
Your resistance to our glare is but in vain.

Round Trip

Where are the stars ,you wondered at?
The swaggering icons you revered?
False idols you confided in?
Such a long and tired journey from there to
here.

The tattered and moth eaten clothes,
That once hung on boyhood limbs,
Fossilised and cast aside, like ancient and
frozen tears,
Buried beneath the rubble of worn out
years.

The Mermaid

If I were a mermaid,
I would have it both ways.
Cocooned from high-tempered elements,
Basking in Summer's golden rays.

Thick skinned when I chose to,
Sensitive when I wished.
At the bottom of every sparkling ocean,
The top of everybody's dreamtime list.

Fearsome when I wanted,
As gentle as beauty must.
Slippery when wet,
A hardened exterior, resistant to rust.

But who needs "the best of both worlds"?
When we know ,all we have is one.
Our task ,to wrench Light from the clasp of
Darkness.
To colour the faintest rainbow, hiding from
the sun.

Stopwatch

Reeling in the spell of unknowing.
Stretching laughter like elastic,
From one child filled fantasy to another.
Like the squirrel gathering for Summer's
end,
Stealing all that glitters.

In preparation,
For the famine of light to come.
The long winter harvest of longing,
Yet unseen,
Kicking in the womb of my unconscious.

The Good Land

Welcome indeed to this valley,
To this fortress sealed with promise,
To this everlasting peace, this haven of
deliverance.
Embattled as we are in this Great Contest,
Throwing invisible dice on an invisible
table,
Until we are replaced by other hunters of
the elusive.

For those who speak the language of
poetry,
For those who dare translate the rhythm
and the harmony of this shared self
delusion ,
For mad dreamers of tolerance,
For rebels who quest for truth,
For idealists who will never surrender,
There is a forever place for you, in this
Good Land.

One Hundred Thousand Welcomes

Layer upon layer, root, on layered root.
Woodland, gorse, open plain,
Beauty is invisible, in an ancient culture,
When nobody speaks your name.

Who governs us?
Who governs you?
Our freedom is ownership,
An emphatic celebration of all that is true.

Where are you from?
How long are you here?
Never a matter of principle,
Your native difference is what I fear.

What are you thinking?
How far can you see?
I will cry for you,
If you can laugh with me.

Hanging Tough

The anxiety society,
That's where I belong,
All the latest designer labels,
Leopard skin thong.

I'm a sporting fellow,
Drinking cider in the park,
The inner self is brooding,
He only gets out after dark.

Like a jungle feline,
I eliminate the weak,
With a fully loaded grimace,
Nobody calls me *"geek"*

Apprentice to an attitude,
Of greed and of distaste,
The consumer age of avarice,
Split forehead, smashed face.

To hell with education,
To those who speak it's name,
To the fools who died for the sake of
freedom,
I'm going to live for the sake of shame.

Playback

The street he commandeered,
With his solid walking cane,
An earthy face of a million passions,
Like prairie bison, hunted in vain.
Far away places were in his eyes,
Long dead lovers, lonely skies.
His tryst was wisdom,
His weapons were words,
From a wizened and toothless mouth
An exalted symphony surged.
Transmitted history with every touch,
Gifts of verbal snapshots,
Bellowed in a hush.
Of barefooted children in the summer rain,
Classroom brutality, I shared his pain.
Bare-knuckle street fighters armed to the
teeth,
With honour and conviction, foreign to
deceit.
Crossly tenders and dawn arrests,
Eucharistic congress, economic tests.
The hungry decades when thousands fled,
Death by consumption, hearts that bled.
A well kept secret not revealed,
His very own golden rule.

Nine and a half decades of ordinary genius,
Draped across a frail, crumpled body,
Like some rare, and sought after, sparkling
jewel.

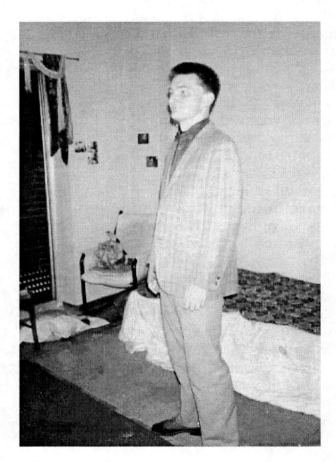

Hidden Eye

The painter's eye converges ,
On moving matter and still life.
All the shapes combine to blink together.
The painter blinks back .
Richness unfolds and engulfs all the eyes,
all the colours.

The air is a still ether, where savage souls
are soothed.
Grazing at their oasis like undernourished
bovine .
Gorging themselves on the scented
ceremony,
Of the artist's temperate hand,
As it partners it's chosen brush.

A silent spotlight falls on the perfect
couple,
Waltzing like age old lovers.
Bristling, beaming, bedazzling,
Gliding timelessly, in graceful dance,
Across the scarlet canvas.

Love's First Song

Garlic wafting it's way up memory lane,
Gushing like purely charged emotion.
Leaking out from the Neon proclamation
announcing "Paul's Pizzas",
The pulsating centrepiece of this leafy
suburban street.

A long established teenage sanctum,
Where once, ancient tribes of leather clad
rockers,
Kissed their sweethearts with salt and
vinegar laden lips.
Be Bop lovers reeled in the arms of jukebox
liberation.
The years had altered little in this little
tributary of creation,
A generation on, floating through an ample
adolescence,
Where I pressed lips for the very first time,
Finding escape in "space invaders" and
"new wave" angst.

But passion is timeless, it has the same
taste,
Passion has the same feel,
It has its own smell,
Passion has the hunger to heal.
From fractured childhoods to dislocated
mature years,
No matter who or what may fall, beneath
the reaper's unholy scythe.
Love's heartbeats are timeless,
They never rest.

And now,
No more salt and vinegar rockabilly,
No more pumped up "new wave",
But rather, chimes of a new era.
Dance, trance and hip hop,
Television advertisement jingles,
From take-away to takeout,
Cellular and cordless.

The rhythm is the same as it always was.
Voices in high-pitched unison,
Mad with youth, in excited anticipation,
As they embark on the journey.
Hostages forever,
Like all of us before them,
Powerless to resist,
The wonderful promise of Love's first song.

The Unfortunate Cup of Tea

It's not just the tea, but what it lies in,
Cracked, chipped, and stained, in
memoriam to some past sin.
This cloudy broth in a jaded cup,
Like an infant presented to a sacrificial slab
Supported by spindly metatarsals,
And the reluctant muscles of a bony wrist,
As the prized beverage is held aloft,
To the fading early evening light.

Here in the confines of this porcelain
receptacle,
Moored safely away from raging sentiment,
Perched upon a navy coloured coaster,
A monster heart wrangles furiously.
Heads bowed as if in prayer,
One steely eye blinks.
A breath is exhaled.
For a mile-second, there is a fleeting recall
to serenity.

This cup is then jerked suddenly from its
resting place,
Transported by a dainty and manicured
hand,
Forced against lips unyielding.
The tongue breaks ranks, and reaches out
for the tempting aromatic.
Taste buds rejoice, and trigger eye lashes to
lift.
Like Mediaeval armies on the eve of battle,
The emerald green rapaciously searches
the light blue,
For some secret signal.

Lightning Strikes

The pleasure bell resounded,
In a perfect pitch
Of past pleasures
Two spirits are one,
The search is re-run.
Open the floodgates,
Don't hold back the tide
In love there is no legislator,
By which we must abide.

There are no truths but one,
Above our earth
Under our sun.
Our fates belong to another
We are brother,
Sister, father, mother.
Forgotten faces are distant places
The heart wanders paths,
It retraces.
Seeking sanctuary unabated,
Origin blue, destination elated.

In one fond kiss, remember this:
That in love-Time stands still.
Our voices shrill,
Are heard as one.
What is this beauty
That we have spun?

DEPARTURE

Fellowship forged,
In the corner of a besieged fortress.
Was this the reason,
Mary ripped Philip's heart out?
That day in the Family Court,
He was so thirsty he could have drunk her
tears.
But they were out of reach.

In the spring of life,
There are kaleidoscopes,
Through which all lovers gaze,
Looking for the rainbow.
The kaleidoscope Mary bought Philip
blinded him.
Their love was now an ancient empire,
And love's ruins were on display,
In this desert where Philip's lips parched.

Then suddenly,
Tundra-like, the heart that once bleated,
The unfettered passions of a child,
Whose seeds were sown,
Flooded his memory,
Like displaced persons,
Searching for a home.

Love's merry-go-round, forever keeps on
spinning.
Losers hang on thinking they're winning.
On a clear day from a distance,
Breaking hearts,
 At the point of least resistance.
An outside view is victorious in defeat.
 Far from this fairground,
Philip chases love ,down a one way street.

Shadow Boxing

The flickering light pounded on his face,
A face peering longingly into the future,
Yearning for wisdoms not yet visited.
It's attachment had no such ambition,
Content in a sinewy frame and angular
motion,
Jumping to every heartbeat,
Impatient for the next.

Layered thin lips,
Circling the smallest most sanguine orifice.
Eyes deep set, and rigorous,
As if summoning up some ancient native
energy.
Cheekbones and forehead conspicuous in
high symphony.
The nose, granite like and determined,
Chiseled from Mount Rushmore.

The body always in tune, its repertoire
unchanging,
Bittersweet, shameless, tingling,
Striving to reach the highest notes,
Ravishing and ravished.
Yet this corpus like a beautiful and
demented mother,
Could not entice her lofty offspring,
To suck upon the teat,
To taste her orchid's rancid emission.

RAINBOW'S END

Like a boomerang dispatched, to fly on
severed wing,
A scavenger's life to eke out, beneath a
foreign city's din.
From the Severn Bridge to Tyneside,
Carlisle to Penzance,
The rebel heart of exile, seeking friendship
in every glance.

A talented hand turned to everything,
Sweat, welts, and deeply held scars.
Millionaire and Pauper, five million
reasons.
Nightly crucifixion in tobacco stanched
bars.

Not the love of a woman nor commercial
greed,
Did your gentle soul trespass.
But a towering passion that you poured,
Into the bottom of every glass.

The semi-circle completed,
You have returned to your dispatch,
No crock of gold, no harem here,
No dreams left alive, to hatch.

Cardboard is your groundsheet,
A blanket of frost bitten stars.
Bitter memories, failed futures,
Ancestral curses, resonant from afar.

City of the Dead

Living ghosts snare us with their dreams,
Long since dead.
Staggering through streets,
Unrecognisable.
Wandering frantically,
Through the eye of this needle,
The leader,
And the led.

Their colours have faded now,
In beating hearts, that once bled.
Shabbily dressed,
In grey stained overcoats.
Their epitaphs are written,
By self appointed consuls,
In their city of the dead.

Like Pompeii of old,
Their past is on show.
Suffocated by the molten eruption,
Frozen.

But listen,
Listen to that scoundrel heartbeat.
Stubbornly pulsating,
Through the stench of ignoble Centuries.
Listen to the crippled and vacuous talk
Of "Rare Old Times".

Listen to the senseless jibe of septic lovers,
To armchair "experts",
Lying prostrate,
Between the lupine jaws,
Of informed truth.
Irreverence is their bed,
In fevered delirium,
In their very own City of the Dead.

Face to Face

Many have asked . . .
What does it mean?
To see.....
To say "I do".

For those who know....
Silence.....
For fear of others.....
Choose a safer way.

Expansion of thought....
Limitless.....
This sacrificial Lamb ....
Has died -for an empty purpose.

That there is a beginning...
With no end ....
Is doubtless reason.....
For those who question.

It's better to give than receive...
Hurt....

Our daily bread will always come..
A captor from the setting sun.

Like primitive man....
A limited, bordered, world....
Our shield.....
Against failure that is real.

It's been said....
That good is bad....
White is black.....
Happy is sad.

This secret....
Nobody knows.....
Yet everybody speaks.
Of "poetry and prose".

My Mother is in love with Gregory Peck

Somewhere between baking soda and
potato cake,

Between a clear skinned handsome
brunette,
And her baby faced bespectacled little boy.

Between a father's reactionary mantra,
And a brother's boorish devotion to his
master.

Between a watery Winter Irish sun,
And the churning green earth below,
Gasping for expression.

Between the greyness of an austere
rhythmic monotony,
And the blazing yellow of its masterful
Creator.

Between mute heartbeats,
And tortured minds,
Between dying dreams,
And living obsessions,
Lies undiscovered treasure,
On the Snows of Kilamanjaro.

Inner Sanctum

Deep within the night, moonless and
frostbitten,
One lone light bulb was tirelessly spinning
its web,
Abandoned, wearisome, but still turned on.
Cut adrift amidst a sea of darkened
windows,
Of sleeping hungers, of numbed emotions
and chilling dreams,
All in safe moorings for the night.

Might it be a beacon of old?
Guiding this intrepid mariner safely to
shore?
Or a wrecker's torch,
Baiting me towards untold peril?
What secrets lay under this light's tutelage?

From a distance,
Vague contours could be seen.
Darting to and fro, like mayflies,
In this little box of light,
Menacing, at the same time fragile.

Encased in this vast Georgian tomb,
Of one hundred blackened spaces,
I wondered how long and for whom,
This light was shining,
Through all the precious and the forgotten
years.

What dramas lost to history were still being
acted out,
Within the confines of this antiquated little
room?
Enchanted as it seemed, secure,
In the firm grip of Time's passionate
embrace.
If restless spirits were pleading,
Then I was all ears.

ONE VOICE

Through the swamps, the raging mire,
The deafening sound of cannon,
The rank smell of gunpowder,
I can hear your plea.

With the taste of vomit in your mouth,
The sticky feel of dried blood
Covering your spindly corpus like a blanket
You still know you are alive
Every sinewy particle of pain reminds you
Of that reality.
I can hear your plea.

A million a decade of human wrecks,
Corpses lying in fever sheds
Corpses huddled on foundering decks
Shroud less dead on their rocky beds;
Nerve and muscle, heart and brain
Lost to Ireland, lost in vain.
I can hear your plea.

Pause, and you can almost hear
The sounds echo down the ages,
The creak of the burial cart,
The rattle of the hinged coffin door.
The sigh of spade on earth —
All day long, and forever more,
I can hear your plea.

You have given so much,
Waited so long,
Prayed so deeply,
Cried too often,
Laughed too little,
Yet you had no greater pain
Than forging a nation's will in vain.
I can hear your plea.

Centuries came, centuries were spent
In timeless wonderment at what heaven
had sent.
Your story is not over yet.
A vision, forever resting in Thee.
Many in this garden have denied you.
I will always hear your plea.

STRANGER

There are cracks in the plaster, holes in the roof.
The door shouts loudly, but our man is aloof.

He talks to the animals one by one.
He could be crazy because he's lost his tongue.

He's going nowhere, his life is framed.
Yet he fears the future in a cup that is stained.

The past is a pleasure that only he can feel.
Life is illusory, nothing is real.

Protected by a shroud, he walks on a cloud.
His life is a shrine, enraptured by wine.

He harbours a dream, an image that's
sacred.
If he can't obtain this, then he's going to
fake it.

He pays for being different, he knows this
too well.
But the pain is worth it, he's escaped
through hell.

In this lost cause he is always a winner.
In life and in death forever—a sinner.

HOMEWARD

Timepieces of grey granite,
Dripping with ancient spilt blood,
Washed by centuries of driving rain,
Conceal uncivil family feuds,
Imperial genocide,
Benign spirits,
Of the cutthroat pirate and *raparee*.

I am the Centaur, hunter and hunted,
My bones have filled this black earth,
Before language itself was invented.
Delirious with the deafening weeping,
Of human and animal,
Their pleas ignored, their union
consummated,
In this un-consecrated, sacred ground.

The lake is my mirror, to which I genuflect,
Paying homage in the lapping water, to a
timeless Gaelic face.
As the years ebb back and forth, from this
bare mountain pass,
To dense woodland, gliding spear and alien
tongue,
To the holy oak, wild wolfhound and pagan
axe,
When Nature nestled it's bristly back,
Against the hairy bosom of the wondrous
cave dweller.

A distant place in foreign time,
Where my ancestors hunted in the valley
below,
Not yet their fate to be sold into slavery,
Hostages to cruel history,
Their world bordered by the moon and the
sun,
The stars and seasons, their technology.
So many had passed along this path,
Plundered by time's unyielding appetite.
The long journey ahead,
Who was laying in wait for this spirit's
return?

Southbound

The high ceiling of blue laughs down on us,
On our retreat from the frozen landscape.
The cell door lies closed behind.
We are fugitives now,
Forever hopeful, of lush and temperate
terrain ahead.

The light drives us on,
Each heartbeat riding shotgun for the other,
Through twisting turning roads,
Of soft spoken words and secrets shared,
As He guides us forever closer.

Top of the Morning

A gentle breeze from the West
Slowly and carefully releases me,
Into the arms of soft rain drops,
Whole and Refreshed.
Life and death are now as one.
Sensual seductive Nature is enraptured,
Resplendent in the silent humdrum.

The corncrake is busy, as is the blackbird,
With the badger, snipe and brown field
mouse,
Beside the holiest grazing herd.
Mist and moor land, the march hare in full
flight,
In this quietude that is morning,
All creatures fly their kite.

Their constitution lasts forever,
With no amendments sought.
Equality is but a simple grace,
It is never sold nor bought.
Decay and desolation, forever so far away.
Resurgence of a restless spirit at the
breaking of the day.

ISBN 1412029139-9